For Dr Clanan's kids—
Remember the Rainbow!
EBSmith
8/98

Please leave in <u>waiting room</u>!

What
Is
Love?

VLB Veronica Lane Books

What Is Love?

by Etan Boritzer *illustrated* by Robbie Marantz

Veronica Lane Books

513 Wilshire Blvd #282, Santa Monica, CA 90401, USA (800) 651.1001

Library of Congress Cataloging-In-Publication Data
        Boritzer, Etan, 1950-
        What Is Love?

Library of Congress Catalog Card Number 93-94066

Summary: The author presents various points of view for children on themes of goodwill and tolerance.

ISBN 0-9637597-2-8 (bound) ISBN 0-9637597-3-6 (pbk.)

1. Love - Comparative studies - Juvenile Literature 152.41
    I. Marantz, Robbie, 1956-   I. Title

Special Thanks, The Lifschutz Family

Printed in Hong Kong by Primaz Production Ltd.

...To the children
of the world...

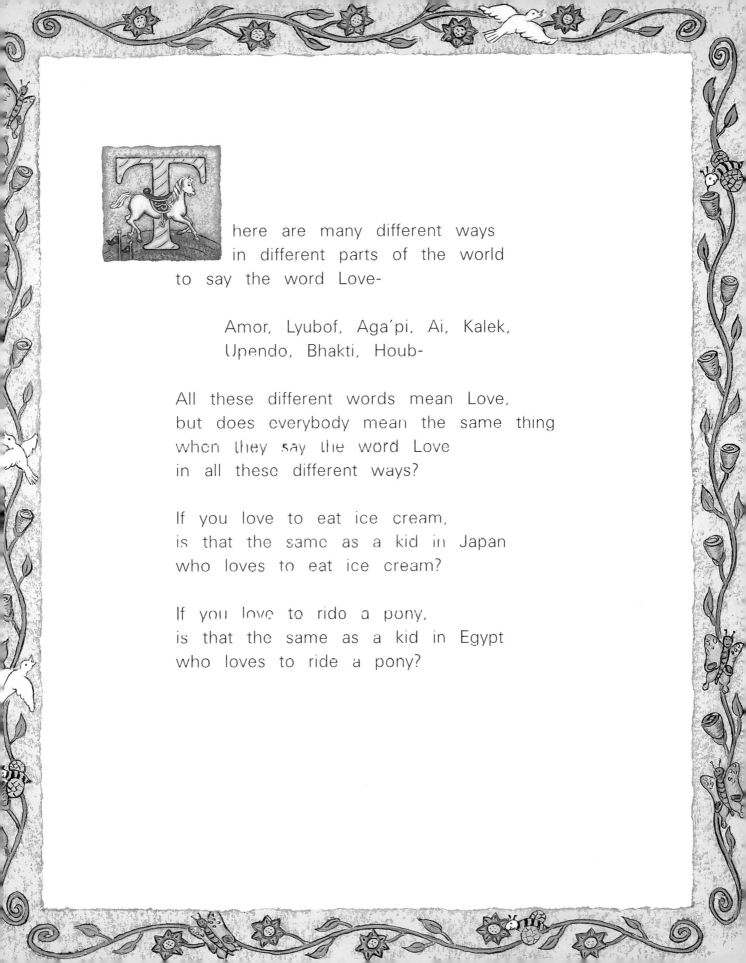

here are many different ways
in different parts of the world
to say the word Love-

Amor, Lyubof, Aga'pi, Ai, Kalek,
Upendo, Bhakti, Houb-

All these different words mean Love,
but does everybody mean the same thing
when they say the word Love
in all these different ways?

If you love to eat ice cream,
is that the same as a kid in Japan
who loves to eat ice cream?

If you love to ride a pony,
is that the same as a kid in Egypt
who loves to ride a pony?

hat is Love ?

What does Love look like?
Is it pink or blue,
or does it have stripes
and polka dots?

Does Love have a taste?
Does it taste like a juicy orange,
or like a chocolate birthday cake?
Does Love taste like green spinach?

What does Love feel like?
Is it warm and furry like a puppy dog?
Or does Love feel freezing cold and tingly
like a snow storm in the mountains?

Does Love have a sound?
Does it sound like a little baby laughing,
or like a big lion roaring in the zoo?

Does Love have a smell?
Does it smell like cookies
baking in the oven,
or like a bright red rose
in a garden, after the rain has stopped?

Maybe Love is not something
you can touch or taste or smell
or see or hear.
Maybe you can only feel Love—
maybe Love is a *feeling*.

But what kind of feeling?
There are outside feelings,
like feeling hot in the summertime,
or like feeling your mouth on fire
if you eat very spicy food.
Or like feeling the soft, wet nose of a pony.

But those are outside feelings
Love is an *inside* feeling.

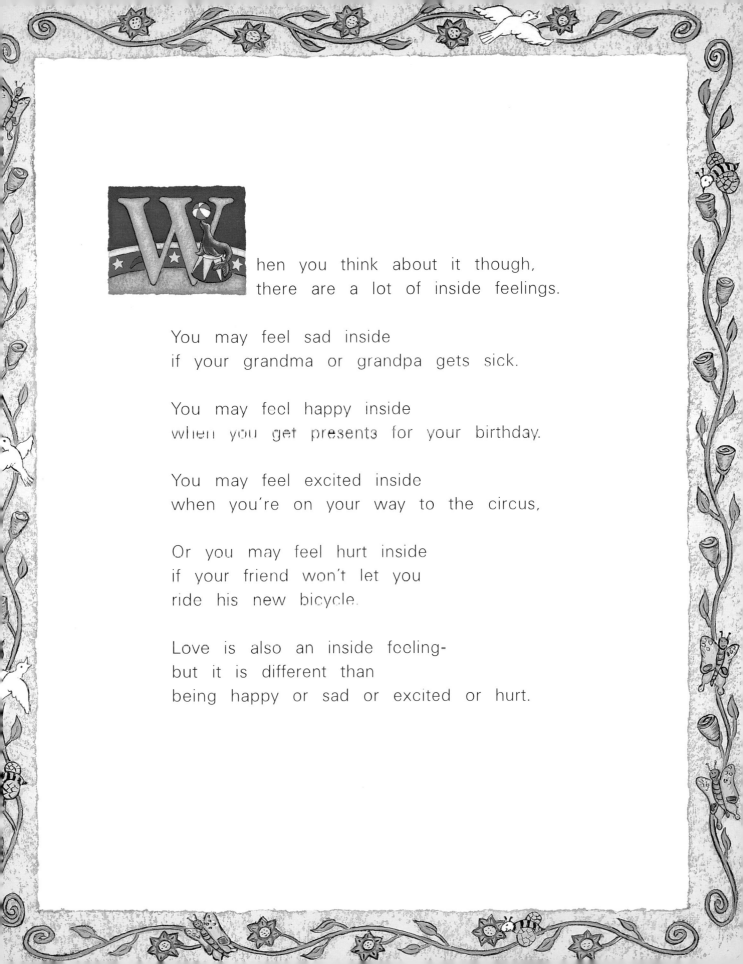

hen you think about it though,
there are a lot of inside feelings.

You may feel sad inside
if your grandma or grandpa gets sick.

You may feel happy inside
when you get presents for your birthday.

You may feel excited inside
when you're on your way to the circus,

Or you may feel hurt inside
if your friend won't let you
ride his new bicycle.

Love is also an inside feeling-
but it is different than
being happy or sad or excited or hurt.

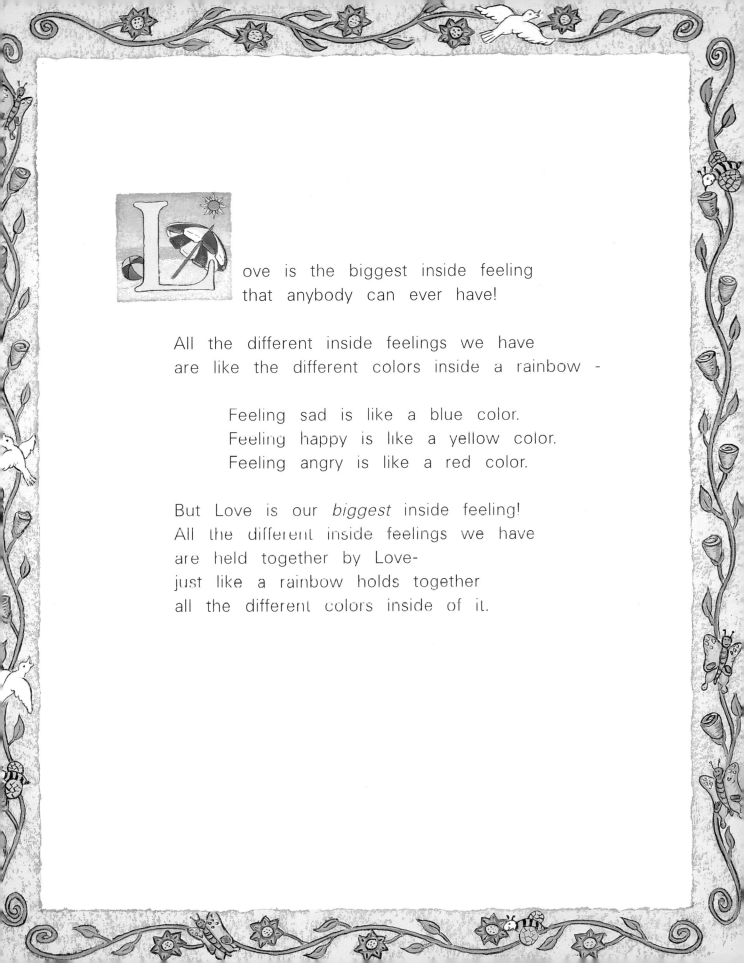

Love is the biggest inside feeling
that anybody can ever have!

All the different inside feelings we have
are like the different colors inside a rainbow -

Feeling sad is like a blue color.
Feeling happy is like a yellow color.
Feeling angry is like a red color.

But Love is our *biggest* inside feeling!
All the different inside feelings we have
are held together by Love-
just like a rainbow holds together
all the different colors inside of it.

ove is like a rainbow
which has all the different colors
going in and out of each other-
all at the same time.

Did you ever see a real rainbow?
It's hard to tell where one color starts
and then mixes into the next color-

the red turns into orange,
which turns into yellow,
which turns to green,
which turns to blue,
and on and on like that.

All those different colors
are held together in one big, beautiful rainbow-
just like all our different inside feelings
are held together by that one big feeling called-
Love!

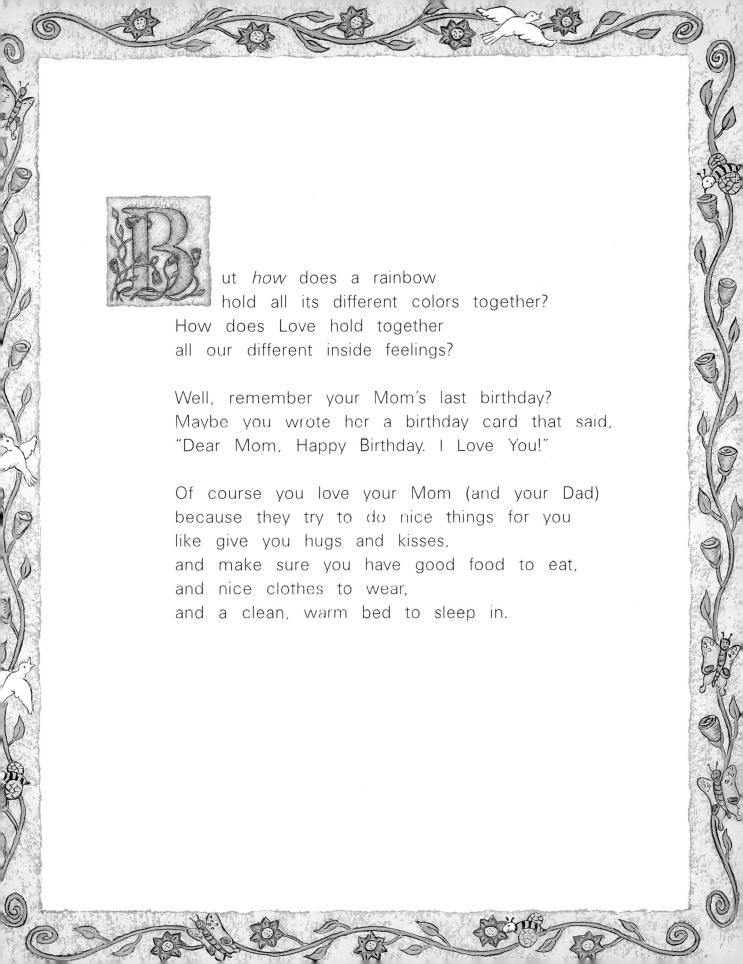

ut *how* does a rainbow
hold all its different colors together?
How does Love hold together
all our different inside feelings?

Well, remember your Mom's last birthday?
Maybe you wrote her a birthday card that said,
"Dear Mom, Happy Birthday. I Love You!"

Of course you love your Mom (and your Dad)
because they try to do nice things for you
like give you hugs and kisses,
and make sure you have good food to eat,
and nice clothes to wear,
and a clean, warm bed to sleep in.

ut sometimes you may feel angry
at your Mom or Dad because
they want you to do things
you don't want to do-
like eat a vegetable that you don't like,
or wear big, warm clothes in winter,
or go to bed early during school.

But you know that your Mom and Dad
want you to eat that vegetable,
so that you will grow up strong and healthy.
And they want you to wear
those big, warm winter clothes,
so you won't catch a cold.
And they want you to go to bed early,
so you will be able to learn at school.

Maybe you feel a little angry
because you don't want to do
what your Mom and Dad tell you to do.
But deep down inside,
you still really love your Mom and Dad,
because you know that they really love you
and you are the most important person
in the world to them!

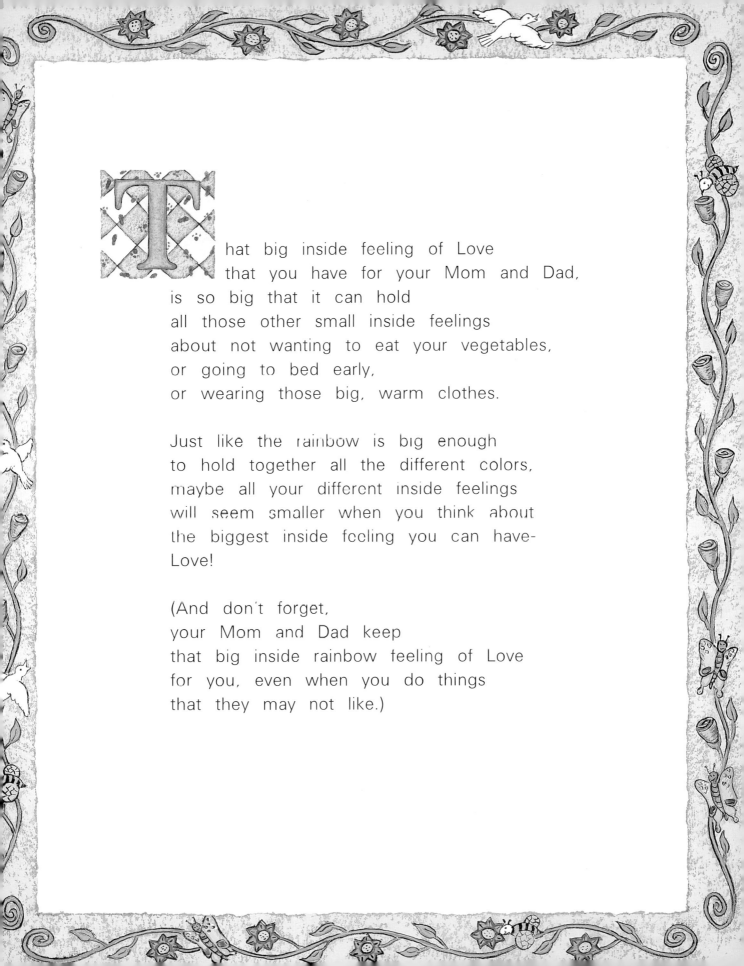

That big inside feeling of Love
that you have for your Mom and Dad,
is so big that it can hold
all those other small inside feelings
about not wanting to eat your vegetables,
or going to bed early,
or wearing those big, warm clothes.

Just like the rainbow is big enough
to hold together all the different colors,
maybe all your different inside feelings
will seem smaller when you think about
the biggest inside feeling you can have-
Love!

(And don't forget,
your Mom and Dad keep
that big inside rainbow feeling of Love
for you, even when you do things
that they may not like.)

That big inside rainbow feeling of Love
is easy to feel for your Mom and Dad,
and your brother or sister,
and your best friend,
or your puppy dog.

But can you feel
that big inside rainbow feeling of Love
for someone who has a different skin color
than you do?

Can you feel
that big inside rainbow feeling of Love
for someone who goes
to a different church or temple
than you do?
Or for someone who doesn't have a home,
or is sick, or can't walk?

It is easy to feel
that big inside rainbow feeling of Love
for your family or friends,
or for things that are close to you.

But maybe you could try to feel
that big inside rainbow feeling of Love
for people or things that are not close to you,
or that you don't understand or like right away.

How can you do that?
How can you feel
that big inside rainbow feeling of Love
for all the people and things
that are different
from the people and things
you know and understand?

It's easy!
Try to remember that all people,
no matter what their skin color,
or what church or temple they go to,
or if they have a home or not,
or are sick-
everybody has the same inside feelings
that you have!

If you fall down,
and scratch your knee,
you may start to cry-
just like every boy or girl in the world
may start to cry,
if he or she falls down
and scratches a knee.

And just like you feel better
when your Mom makes the hurt go away,
every boy and girl in the world
also feels better when his or her Mom
makes the hurt go away.

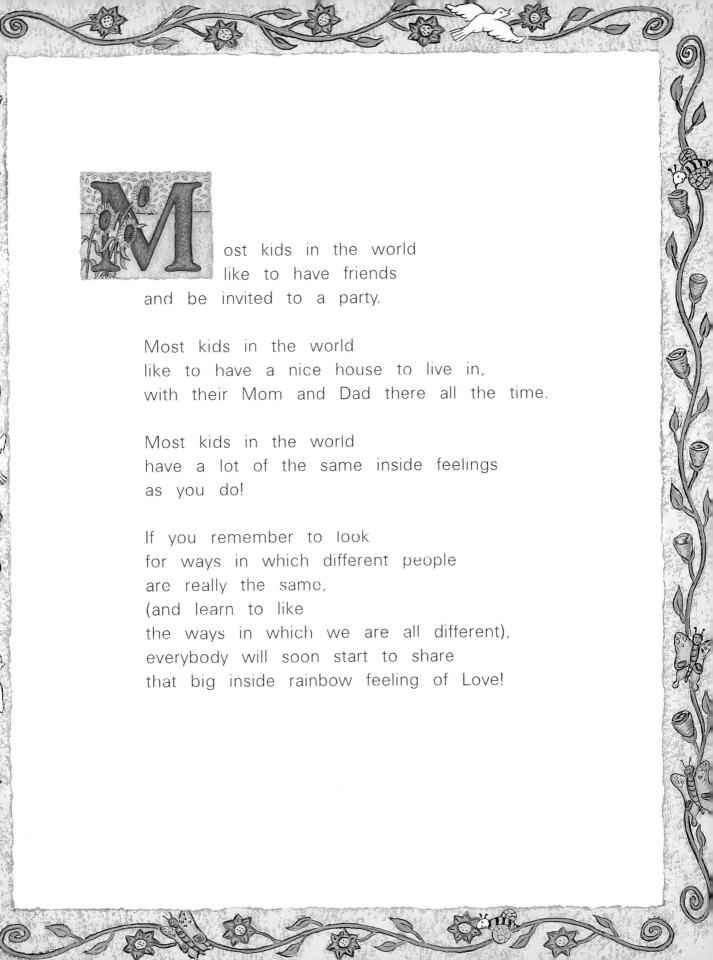

Most kids in the world
like to have friends
and be invited to a party.

Most kids in the world
like to have a nice house to live in,
with their Mom and Dad there all the time.

Most kids in the world
have a lot of the same inside feelings
as you do!

If you remember to look
for ways in which different people
are really the same,
(and learn to like
the ways in which we are all different),
everybody will soon start to share
that big inside rainbow feeling of Love!

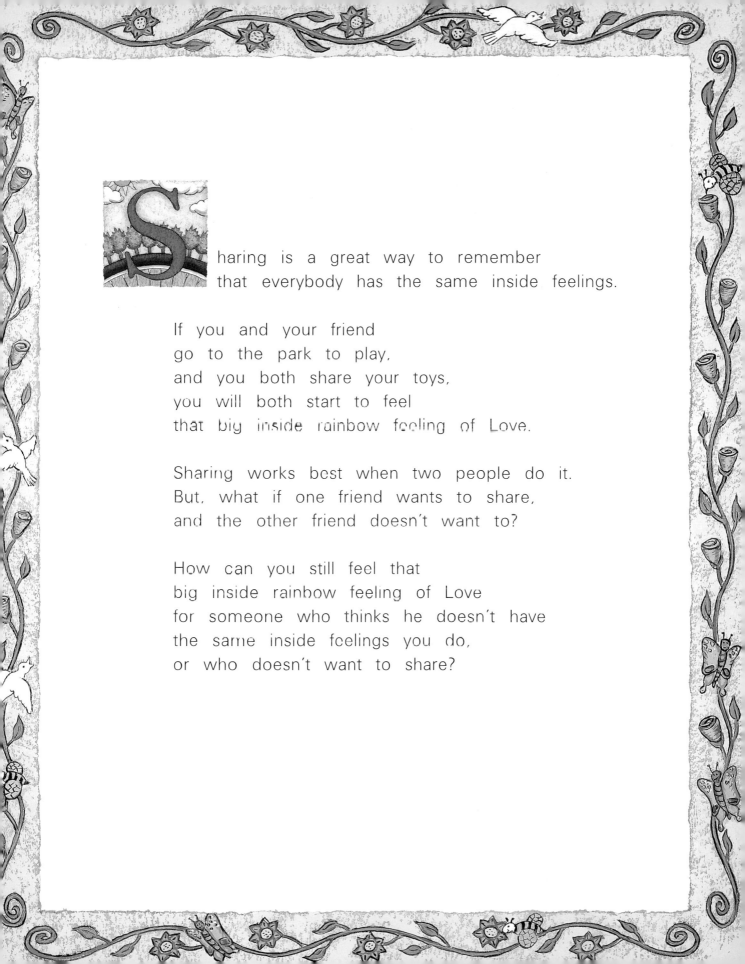

Sharing is a great way to remember
that everybody has the same inside feelings.

If you and your friend
go to the park to play,
and you both share your toys,
you will both start to feel
that big inside rainbow feeling of Love.

Sharing works best when two people do it.
But, what if one friend wants to share,
and the other friend doesn't want to?

How can you still feel that
big inside rainbow feeling of Love
for someone who thinks he doesn't have
the same inside feelings you do,
or who doesn't want to share?

If that happens to you,
you may feel hurt or angry,
and you may not want to play
with that friend anymore.

But instead, try to remember
that big inside rainbow feeling of Love-
maybe you could offer to share
one of *your* toys with him!

Your friend might be so surprised
that you still want to share with him,
that he might also start to feel
that big inside rainbow feeling of Love-

And then, maybe, he'll also want
to start sharing *his* toys with you.

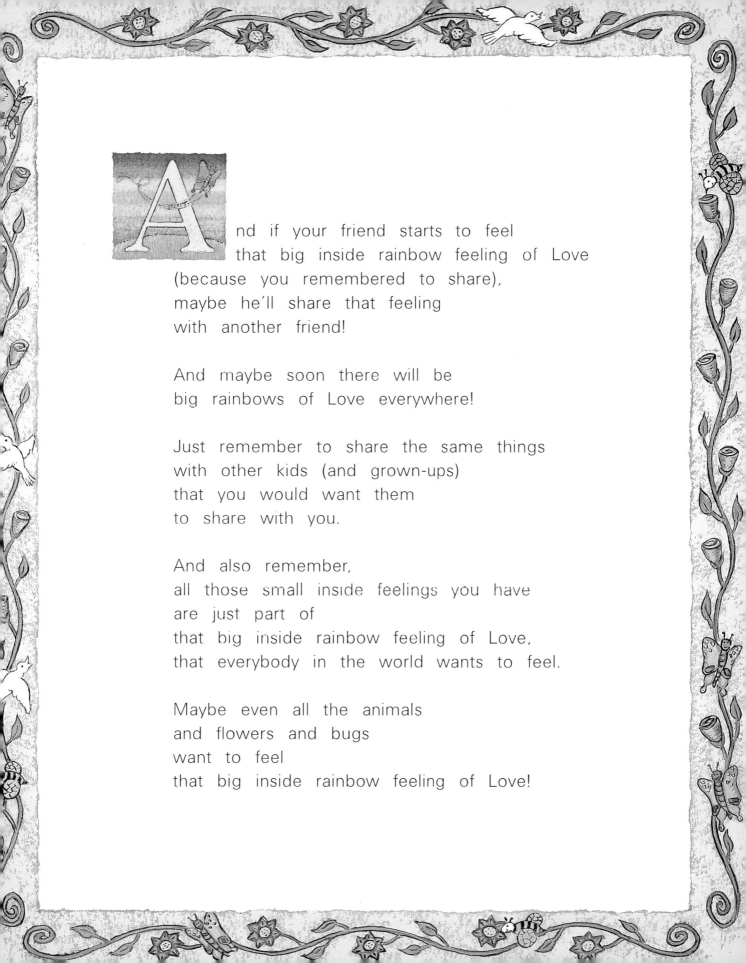

And if your friend starts to feel
that big inside rainbow feeling of Love
(because you remembered to share),
maybe he'll share that feeling
with another friend!

And maybe soon there will be
big rainbows of Love everywhere!

Just remember to share the same things
with other kids (and grown-ups)
that you would want them
to share with you.

And also remember,
all those small inside feelings you have
are just part of
that big inside rainbow feeling of Love,
that everybody in the world wants to feel.

Maybe even all the animals
and flowers and bugs
want to feel
that big inside rainbow feeling of Love!